TAKING A STAND AGAINST THE ENEMY:

Learn How to Experience Victory in Christ Jesus

Kevin L. Zadai

TAKING A STAND AGAINST THE ENEMY

© Copyright 2021 Kevin L. Zadai

All rights reserved. This book is protected by the copyright laws of the United States of America. This book may not be copied or reprinted for commercial gain or profit. The use of short quotations or the copying of an occasional page for personal or group study is permitted and encouraged. Permission will be granted upon request.

Unless otherwise indicated, Scripture quotations are taken from the New King James Version. Copyright © 1982 by Thomas Nelson, Inc. Used by permission. All rights reserved.

Scripture quotations marked (AMPC) are taken from the Amplified® Bible (AMPC), Copyright © 1954, 1958, 1962, 1964, 1965, 1987 by The Lockman Foundation Used by permission. www.Lockman.org.

All Scripture quotations marked (KJV) are taken from the King James Version. Public Domain.

Scripture quotations marked (NLT) are taken from the Holy Bible, New Living Translation, copyright ©1996, 2004, 2015 by Tyndale House Foundation. Used by permission of Tyndale House Publishers, a Division of Tyndale House Ministries, Carol Stream, Illinois 60188. All rights reserved.

Scripture quotations marked (AMP) are taken from the Amplified Bible, Copyright © 1954, 1958, 1962, 1964, 1965, 1987 by The Lockman Foundation. Used by permission. www.Lockman.org.

Please note that Warrior Notes publishing style capitalizes certain pronouns in Scripture that refer to the Father, Son, and Holy Spirit, which may differ from some publishers' styles. Take note that the name "satan" and related names are not capitalized. We choose not to acknowledge him, even to the point of violating accepted grammatical rules. All emphasis within Scripture quotations is the author's own.

Cover design: Virtually Possible Designs
Editing by Lisa Thompson at www.writebylisa.com

For more information about our school, go to www.warriornotesschool.com.
Reach us on the internet: www.Kevinzadai.com

ISBN 13 TP: 9798717473057

TAKING A STAND
AGAINST THE ENEMY

INTRODUCTION

The Lord desires that we understand and war a good fight against our enemy, the devil. Even the apostle Paul reminds us that we are not ignorant of satan's devices. "Lest Satan should get an advantage of us: for we are not ignorant of his devices" (2 Corinthians 2:11). Paul assumes that the reader knows the battle strategies of the enemy.

The idea of having battle strategies and waging war was introduced and reinforced to Timothy, who was being spiritually fathered by Paul. Paul told Timothy, "This charge and admonition I commit in trust to you, Timothy, my son, in accordance with prophetic intimations which I formerly received concerning you, so that inspired and aided by them you may wage the good warfare, holding fast to faith (that leaning of the entire human personality on God in absolute trust and confidence) and having a good (clear) conscience. By rejecting and thrusting from them [their conscience], some individuals have made shipwreck of their faith" (1 Timothy 1:17–18 AMPC).

My heart for every believer in this book is that they understand and implement the strategies of God's warfare in the days ahead. We will see such victory as we come together in unity of the faith and walk in the love of God, standing firm in His will. After all, the Lord is a mighty Warrior, and He never loses. (See Zephaniah 3:17.) He will surely come to your aid.

Enjoy the book!

Kevin L. Zadai

TAKING A STAND
AGAINST THE ENEMY

You Can Enforce the Victory

1

*Having disarmed principalities and powers,
He made a public spectacle of them,
triumphing over them in it.*
—Colossians 2:15

It sounds threatening, doesn't it, that people want to start a war with the devil. However, the thing about it is that satan is already waging war against all of us. He is waging war against the saints and trying to wear us down. We can turn the tables on our enemy and start a war with the devil that we can win. I like to give the devil a hard time, and I want to teach you how to do the same. I have picked ten different points that I feel are very important for you to use and implement in your life. I want you to feel the victory, see the victory, experience the victory, and know the victory you have in Jesus Christ.

"And you, being dead in your trespasses and the uncircumcision of your flesh, He has made alive together with Him, having forgiven you all trespasses, having wiped out the handwriting of requirements that was against us, which was contrary to us. And He has taken it out of the way, having nailed it to the cross. Having disarmed principalities and powers, He made a public spectacle of them, triumphing over them in it" (Colossians 2:13–15).

Jesus made a show of the devil openly, and He triumphed over him on the cross, and you, too, can enforce that victory. You have to realize that Jesus came, and the whole plan was to destroy the works of the devil. Jesus is doing that for you—doing it continually. You need to recognize that and think about it all the time. The Spirit of the Lord is always willing to take you to your next step.

"Trust in the Lord with all your heart, and lean not on your own understanding; in all your ways acknowledge Him, and He shall direct your paths" (Proverbs 3:5–6). You need to rely on the Word of God. However, the Holy Spirit must have His way to reveal strategies that have been given to us so that we can enforce the victory on this earth. The Lord has given me specific strategies, found in the Word of God. However, we need to experience these and walk them out. We need an encounter with the Word instead of just reading it.

TAKING A STAND AGAINST THE ENEMY

The Spirit of God must become so real in our lives that He takes the Word of God and makes it alive, and we experience Him. That is called experiential knowledge and not just head knowledge.

In addition to the Spirit, we must have understanding. We can pray in the Spirit all day, but at some point, we must engage God with our understanding as well. There is a balance to this, and the enemy wants to pull you into his ring or into his way of doing things so that he can win against you. The devil knows that he cannot win against you in God's ring.

If you stay in the Word of God and the Spirit of God and fortify yourself with what God has given us through Jesus Christ, then the enemy has no way of winning against you. I saw that the devil will bother Christians on earth, no matter what they do. A great majority of Christians think that if they stay out of sight, keep a low profile, do not rattle the cage, so to speak, and do not make any waves, then the devil will leave them alone. It is just not true because satan wants to wear out the saints. "And he shall speak great words against the most High, and shall wear out the saints of the most High, and think to change times and laws: and they shall be given into his hand until a time and times and the dividing of time" (Daniel 7:25 KJV).

You can do ten different things to start a successful war with the devil, which I learned when I was on the other side in heaven. I will address each one of these in this book. God bless you.

PRAYER

Father, in the name of Jesus, I thank You. I thank You, Holy Spirit, that You have Your way of revealing the strategies that you have given us through Jesus Christ so that we can enforce victory on this earth. I thank You for the blood of Jesus. I thank You for the Spirit of God, and I thank You for the name of Jesus. You will cause us to triumph in all things. Father, thank You. In the name of Jesus, we pray. Amen.

TAKING A STAND AGAINST THE ENEMY

What did the Holy Spirit reveal to you regarding this chapter?

TAKING A STAND
AGAINST THE ENEMY

Cooperate with Your Heavenly Help

2

*Praise the Lord, you angels, you mighty ones
who carry out his plans, listening for each of his
commands. Yes, praise the Lord, you armies of
angels who serve him and do his will!*
—Psalm 103:20–21 NLT

The number one way you can start a war with the devil and win is to cooperate with your heavenly help, which is God's angel armies. You have an angel that has been assigned to you. If you cooperate with your angel, you can start a war that you can win against the devil. I will talk about cooperating with your angels and the angel assignments that have been given to you.

Angels are ultrafast, brilliant, and smart. They understand God's ways, and they have been briefed about you. They have a lot of information concerning you and strategies for you, and they want to implement those things in your life. You need to cooperate with your angel!

Everyone has an angel assigned to them, and I saw this when I was in heaven. Even unsaved people still have angels around them. The minute that these people receive the Lord, their angels start to act in a greater way and begin to bring them into the fullness of what God has for them. Before they are saved, their angels are working to bring them to salvation. Angels are constantly leading and guiding people to a place where they hear the gospel or talk to someone who knows about the gospel. The angels coordinate those kinds of meetings with unsaved people.

"But the love of the Lord remains forever with those who fear him. His salvation extends to the children's children of those who are faithful to his covenant, of those who obey his commandments! The Lord has made the heavens his throne; from there he rules over everything" (Psalm 103:17–19 NLT).

"Praise the Lord, you angels, you mighty ones who carry out his plans, listening for each of his commands. Yes, praise the Lord, you armies of angels who serve him and do his will! Praise the Lord, everything he has created, everything in all his kingdom. Let all that I am praise the Lord" (Psalm 103:20–22 NLT).

For your benefit, concentrate and meditate on Psalm 103. You can also read the following verse. "Who makes His

TAKING A STAND
AGAINST THE ENEMY

angel spirits, His ministers a flame of fire." (See Psalm 104:4.) These angels have been sent to minister to those who inherit salvation. They are flames of fire that have been assigned to you, and they are so fast that they have to slow down for you to see them. They are on fire and full of God's light.

As a believer, at some point, you will humbly start to accept that you have heavenly hosts or heavenly armies around you. You accept that the angels want to engage with you and help you fulfill your destiny in Christ. That happened to Peter in Acts 12:6–17. This whole story is about Peter, who was being held in a jail cell and was about to go to trial to be put to death by King Herod.

The night before Peter was to stand trial, he fell asleep, chained in the jail cell between two soldiers with guards at the prison gates. Suddenly, a bright light appeared in the cell, and an angel of the Lord stood before Peter. The angel struck Peter on the side to awaken him and said, "Arise quickly!" When he arose, the chains fell off Peter's hands. Then the angel said, "Get dressed and tie your sandals on." After Peter obeyed, the angel said, "Put on your coat and follow me."

Peter followed the angel out of the jail cell without even realizing what was happening. He thought he was having a vision. They passed the first and the second guard posts and came to the iron gate of the city, which opened by itself. They passed through these and onto the street, and then the angel suddenly left him.

When Peter came to his senses, he said, "Now I know for certain that the Lord has sent His angel and has saved me from Herod and all the Jewish leaders," for they had planned to kill him. Peter was shown that he was to go to a certain house, and he found himself standing at the door where they were praying for him. When they opened the door, they thought that they were seeing Peter's angel. They could not believe that he had been set free, even though they were in the house praying for his freedom!

It was such an encouraging time in the early church, and it is the same for us today. What happened to Peter can happen to, you no matter your situation. The angels of the Lord are there, and they can be sent to rescue, lead, and guide you. They can help you find employment and help you with opportunities to put you in the perfect will of God. They can lead you to certain people that you need to see. I have seen this happen so often, not just for myself but for many others.

Engage your angel, and let your angel help you, acknowledging that the Lord has sent His angels. If you do that, you will see supernatural guidance and supernatural events happen every day. No matter what you think you know or don't know, God will teach you. When I thought I didn't know something, the angels led me into God's perfect will for me. Even when I misunderstood the situation, God's angels helped me. They are there for you too.

Like Peter, you might be facing a huge problem and feel as if the devil has you trapped. Remember that the power of

TAKING A STAND AGAINST THE ENEMY

God is with you and in you and that angels are all around you. I always acknowledge my angels and tell them that they are to do the Lord's bidding, whatever He has spoken. I acknowledge their presence and the fact that God has put them on assignment. "For he will order his angels to protect you wherever you go. They will hold you up with their hands so you won't even hurt your foot on a stone" (Psalm 91:11–12 NLT).

The angels are sent on special assignments to ensure that we don't even trip on a stone or stub our toe. Be encouraged that God is with you and that if you want to start a war with the devil, let your angels start to move you into God's perfect will by acknowledging Him in all your ways. (See Proverbs 3:5–6.) Acknowledge that you have heavenly help. The enemy will not win this war when your angelic help works with you. That is the number one way to receive an impartation to engage in war with satan so that he cannot win. The angels are mighty and powerful, but they need you to cooperate with them.

PRAYER

Father, in the name of Jesus, I thank You for this impartation from heaven. I thank You that the reality of angelic help is coming to all my friends worldwide. I pray that they would accept the ministry of angels right now and that they would begin to move with You, Father. I pray that they would work with You for this great move that You are putting on the earth: the move of Your love, Your healing, and Your glory.

I thank You that the angels are involved and on the ground, willing to help. Father, release everyone reading this right now by the power of the Holy Spirit. Let Your angels go forth and minister to those who will inherit salvation and help them in the name of Jesus. Amen.

TAKING A STAND AGAINST THE ENEMY

What did the Holy Spirit reveal to you regarding this chapter?

TAKING A STAND
AGAINST THE ENEMY

Ask God Himself to Show Up

3

*The Lord your God is with you, the Mighty
Warrior who saves. He will take great delight in
you; In his love, he will no longer rebuke you,
but will rejoice over you with singing.*
—Zephaniah 3:17 NIV

The second way the Lord taught me you can start a war with the devil and win is to ask God Himself to show up. You already know what happens when God shows up, and we have seen this all through the Bible. Every time God visited Moses on the mountain, the mountain caught on fire. There were earthquakes, thunder, and all kinds of natural disasters. King David engaged the enemies and won because God was with him in a mighty way.

I want to share with you that if you want to start a war with the devil, the second thing to do is to ask God to show up. When God shows up, He will draw His sword, and as it says in Zephaniah 3:17, "The Lord your God is with you, the Mighty Warrior who saves" (NIV). God is a warrior with a sword that He draws, and He will fight for you.

God will make sure that you win this battle. It will be a permanent win forever because God will have His way when we ask Him to come in. I tell the Lord every day that I invite Him into my life to be with me in every way. I say what Moses said and tell God that if He does not go with us, then we are not going. (See Exodus 33:14–16.)

"I am the vine, you are the branches. He who abides in Me, and I in him, bears much fruit; for without Me you can do nothing" (John 15:5). Jesus said that without Him, we can do nothing because we are connected to the vine. We currently live in difficult times, and we need to ask God to come into every situation.

Jesus once talked to me about this, even about people's finances. He said, "I have a lot of people who need prayer for their finances, and they are always asking questions about their situation." He told me to write a book called *Supernatural Finances*. Jesus said, "My people are having trouble with finances, but they will not let Me into their finances."

We sometimes do that. We think we have a certain situation or certain part of our lives under control. So we say, "Okay,

TAKING A STAND
AGAINST THE ENEMY

I have this, Lord." We ask the Lord to take care of our families and of sickness in our bodies, but we do not let Him into our finances. However, you now need to ask God to come in a mighty way and show up in your house, live fully in your body, and push out sickness, financial problems, and relational problems. The Lord can do this, but you must ask Him. In this way, you can start a war with the devil and win because God will show up.

"The eyes of the Lord watch over those who do right; his ears are open to their cries for help. But the Lord turns his face against those who do evil; he will erase their memory from the earth. The Lord hears his people when they call to him for help. He rescues them from all their troubles. The Lord is close to the brokenhearted; he rescues those whose spirits are crushed. The righteous person faces many troubles, but the Lord comes to the rescue each time" (Psalm 34:15–19 NLT).

I have often been in impossible situations, and I know that the Lord is always ready to act when I cry out to Him for help. I call out for help all the time, and I ask Him to be involved with me, to be in my life in a bigger way every day. If I cannot handle a situation, I ask God to help me. When He shows up, the demons scream and become enraged because you are cooperating with your angels and they come to help you. When you ask God to come into your situation and cooperate with God Himself, the demons become very nervous. It starts a war with the devil because when God shows up, He draws His sword, and the enemy becomes afraid.

"What then shall we say to these things? If God is for us, who can be against us?...Yet in all these things we are more than conquerors through Him who loved us" (Romans 8:31, 37). If God is for us, who can be against us? The answer is no one. You can start a successful war with the devil by asking God to show up. This point is very powerful, and God is with you in a mighty way!

TAKING A STAND AGAINST THE ENEMY

PRAYER

I pray, Father, that You would give the people eyes to see and ears to hear and that You would give them a spirit of boldness. Father, I pray that it would come upon them just as it did when they prayed for boldness to testify in the book of Acts.

I thank You, Lord, that all the people, all my friends worldwide, would ask You to show up. You will war on their behalf. I thank You, Lord, that Your sword is drawn and You will defend Your people right now in the name of Jesus. I break the power of the enemy that has come against you. The Lord says that He wants to walk with you, lead you, guide you, and take your hand. He wants to bring you into what He has for you and that you are not to fear. The Lord is with you in a mighty way. In Jesus's name. Amen.

What did the Holy Spirit reveal to you regarding this chapter?

TAKING A STAND
AGAINST THE ENEMY

Get Over Yourself

4

*And He said to me, "My grace is sufficient
for you, for My strength is
made perfect in weakness."*
—2 Corinthians 12:9

The fourth point is one of my favorites and is a great way to start a war with the devil. You have to get over yourself. Even the apostle Paul had to get over himself, so you are in good company here. As a young man, Paul was trained to teach and be the head Pharisee in the world, and because of that, he had a lot of pride. With all of Paul's learning, he was blind to spiritual matters. Paul had to be humbled by God and get over himself before writing the amazing spiritual words in the Bible that he did.

"And He said to me, 'My grace is sufficient for you, for My strength is made perfect in weakness.' Therefore most gladly I will rather boast in my infirmities, that the power of Christ may rest upon me. Therefore I take pleasure in infirmities, in reproaches, in needs, in persecutions, in distresses, for Christ's sake. For when I am weak, then I am strong." (2 Corinthians 12:9–10).

A spirit had been assigned to Paul, and the devil was attacking him. Every time Paul prayed to God about it, God told him that His grace was sufficient and all that Paul needed and His power worked best in weakness. The Lord kept repeating this. Paul was asking the Lord to take this spirit away, but we have authority in the name of Jesus to tell demons to go. Paul did not understand this.

God was saying that He had already given Paul the ability to remove this spirit. God said that His power worked best in weakness. If Paul had submitted to God and resisted the devil, the devil would have fled from him. (See James 4:7.) Remember, when you start a war with the devil by getting over yourself, the power of God is made manifest in weakness, not in strength.

"So humble yourselves under the mighty hand of God, and at the right time he will lift you up in honor" (1 Peter 5:6–7 NLT). The devil does not want anything to do with you if you are humble because he cannot tempt you. He cannot seduce you because you are not deceived. When we become prideful, we are deceived because pride blinds us.

TAKING A STAND
AGAINST THE ENEMY

Paul said that when Christ's power is revealed in him, it is in his weakness, which is why Paul said that he took pleasure in weaknesses. When Paul endured insults, hardships, persecutions, and troubles, he was suffering for Christ, and when he was weak, he was made strong. I experience this all the time, and the Lord Jesus taught me this to get over myself. It is okay when you feel weak because the Holy Spirit then comes in power and raises you up.

"Likewise the Spirit also helps in our weaknesses. For we do not know what we should pray for as we ought, but the Spirit Himself makes intercession for us with groanings which cannot be uttered. Now He who searches the hearts knows what the mind of the Spirit is, because He makes intercession for the saints according to the will of God." (Romans 8:26–27)

Here in Romans, we see that in our weakness, the Spirit comes in and super-intercedes for us. The Spirit takes hold of us and lifts us up in power so that we pray the perfect will of God. If you think about it, you cannot know what to do or how to do God's perfect will on your own, which is why you are weak. So you rely on the Spirit because then He comes in and lifts you up.

When the Holy Spirit lifts you up, you have resurrection power and pray the perfect will of God by yielding to His Spirit. That is an important key, but it will start a war with the devil. However, the devil cannot win this war against you because you have gotten over yourself.

"Or do you not know that your body is the temple of the Holy Spirit who is in you, whom you have from God, and you are not your own? For you were bought at a price; therefore glorify God in your body and in your spirit, which are God's" (1 Corinthians 6:19–20). Paul told the Corinthians that their bodies were the temple of the Holy Spirit and that their bodies were not their own because they had been bought with a price. Your body houses the Holy Spirit on this earth. The Holy Spirit is inside you if you are a Christian, and your life is not your own. Paul said it was as though Christ had borrowed his body and was working through him. It was as though Jesus was doing His ministry through Paul, and Paul did not have a life of his own.

"For if you live according to the flesh you will die; but if by the Spirit you put to death the deeds of the body, you will live" (Romans 8:13). "I say then: Walk in the Spirit, and you shall not fulfill the lust of the flesh" (Galatians 5:16). You want the devil to know that you have been bought and that you are living your life for Jesus Christ. That will start a war, but these devils cannot win against you.

Enforce the victory that Christ has given you by putting to death the misdeeds of the body. When you yield to the Spirit, you do not fulfill the lusts of the flesh. You cannot please God if you yield to the flesh, but you can please Him if you walk in the Spirit. Sons of God who walk in the Spirit and who yield to the Spirit please God. "For as many as are led by the Spirit of God, these are sons of God" (Romans 8:14).

TAKING A STAND AGAINST THE ENEMY

You are pleasing to God because you have gotten over yourself and all the abilities that you might think you have. You have humbled yourself, and you let God's great power be revealed in you. In these last days, all of you will wage a great war against the enemy, and you will win because you are doing it by the Spirit of God.

PRAYER

Father, in the name of Jesus, I thank You for the impartation of the reality that we have been bought at a price through Jesus Christ. We are not our own, and our bodies are the temple of the Holy Spirit, and we yield our members to You.

Father, we yield and pray that all the abilities that have been given to us in the Spirit come forth in the name of Jesus. I release you right now into the perfect will of God and into the perfect destiny that God has for you. I pray that you stay strong in the Lord and in His mighty power and that you have all things through Jesus Christ. In the name of Jesus, He always causes you to triumph. In Jesus's name. Amen.

TAKING A STAND AGAINST THE ENEMY

What did the Holy Spirit reveal to you regarding this chapter?

TAKING A STAND
AGAINST THE ENEMY

Pray Excessively In The Spirit

5

*I thank my God I speak in tongues
more than any of you.*
—1 Corinthians 14:18 NLT

The fourth way to start a successful war with the devil and win is to constantly pray in the Spirit. Paul said that he prayed in the Spirit, prayed in tongues, more than anyone. This practice will start a war with the devil that you can win. Paul talked about praying in tongues a lot, and Paul was a very learned man.

At one time, Paul did not believe in all these Christian principles and practices, but when he was converted, he flipped over to the other extreme and went all out for the Lord. He prayed in tongues excessively, and I will be like the apostle Paul and be excessive too. I will pray in tongues more than anyone else, and so can you. We are going to pray in tongues as much as we possibly can.

> So anyone who speaks in tongues should pray also for the ability to interpret what has been said. For if I pray in tongues, my spirit is praying, but I don't understand what I am saying.
>
> Well then, what shall I do? I will pray in the spirit, and I will also pray in words I understand. I will sing in the spirit, and I will also sing in words I understand. For if you praise God only in the spirit, how can those who don't understand you praise God along with you? How can they join you in giving thanks when they don't understand what you are saying? You will be giving thanks very well, but it won't strengthen the people who hear you.
>
> I thank God that I speak in tongues more than any of you. (1 Corinthians 14:13–18 NLT)

First Corinthians says here that anyone who speaks in tongues should also pray for the ability to interpret what is being said. Paul is talking about a public assembly where you are around other people in a service and exercising the gift of tongues. Then you should interpret your tongues so that everyone else can understand what you are saying.

However, in your personal prayer life, which is referenced here, you are speaking mysteries unto God. (See verse 2.) Everyone has the ability and the opportunity to accept the

TAKING A STAND
AGAINST THE ENEMY

Holy Spirit in this way. When you are overflowing and speaking in the Spirit, you are speaking in other tongues.

Paul says that the gift of tongues as a gift to the church in the public assembly has to be interpreted. Unless you can interpret or unless someone present can interpret, you should stay quiet in the public assembly. (See 1 Corinthians 14:28.) I can interpret my tongues, and I have the gift of tongues publicly, and I have the gift of interpretation of tongues publicly.

Everyone can pray in the Spirit. In a believers' meeting with no unbelievers present, if we all agree to pray in the Spirit, we can all do so. Then you do not have to interpret because everyone has agreed to pray in the Spirit to God. In a public assembly where we are exercising the gifts and unbelievers are present, someone should interpret what is said if someone speaks in tongues. That way, everyone can participate and be edified. (See 1 Corinthians 14:22–25.)

We should pray in tongues because it is evidence of the personal relationship that we have with the Holy Spirit. "And they were all filled with the Holy Spirit and began to speak with other tongues, as the Spirit gave them utterance" (Acts 2:4). In the book of Acts, every time the Spirit descended on people, they spoke in tongues. That is the initial evidence of being baptized in the Holy Spirit. We need to pray in the Spirit. "But you, beloved, building yourselves up on your most holy faith, praying in the Holy Spirit, keep yourselves in the love of God" (Jude 1:20–21). This practice is very important.

If you want to pick a fight with the devil, praying in tongues will keep him out of what is going on. As Paul said, when you pray in an unknown tongue, your spirit is praying, and you are praying unto God, but your mind is not fruitful. In this private prayer time, you pray in tongues, and you are speaking privately to God by the Holy Spirit. When I am in a public assembly, I interpret my tongues. I publicly pray in tongues, and then I will interpret what is being said, which is what God wants.

I believe that you will now be encouraged to pray in the Spirit all the time. I tell people to block off ten minutes a day to pray in the Spirit and then to pray to yourself in the Spirit in a whisper throughout the day. I did this for thirty years while at my job, and nobody knew what I was doing.

Interestingly, if a person had a devil in them, the devil knew that I was praying silently and would speak up. They would tell me to stop doing that even though I was not speaking audibly. They could hear sounds coming from me. I was praying in my spirit in a whisper, but they would become irritated, and the devils would rise in people and start speaking. That is how I know this gift picks a fight with the devil. This point is vital: if you pray in the Spirit, you will pick a fight with the devil.

You can wage war against the devil by praying in tongues. I will pray right now for you to be baptized in the Holy Spirit if you do not have the baptism of the Holy Spirit and fire with the initial evidence of speaking in tongues. I will pray that the Holy Spirit fills you with Himself right now.

TAKING A STAND
AGAINST THE ENEMY

PRAYER

Father, I release everyone to pray in the Spirit and that they would be filled, built up in their most holy faith, and that they would remain in the love of God.

I thank You, Father, that everyone reading this would receive the Holy Spirit right now in fire, the baptism of fire, and speak by the Spirit. Just let it come through your belly and out of your mouth and your tongue be loosed in the name of Jesus. I thank You, Father, for freedom to speak and to pray in the Spirit in the name of Jesus. I thank You, Father, that where the Spirit of the Lord is, there is freedom.

I thank You that the power of the enemy in everyone's life is broken and that his strategies against my friends are rendered null and void right now in the name of Jesus. I thank you that all those evil spirits are releasing people all over the world and that that they are being baptized in the Holy Spirit and with fire. I feel that so strongly. Receive that as you flow with God. You are flowing in the Holy Spirit. Thank You, Father. Amen.

TAKING A STAND AGAINST THE ENEMY

What did the Holy Spirit reveal to you regarding this chapter?

TAKING A STAND
AGAINST THE ENEMY

Overeat the Word of God

6

*Don't copy the behavior and customs of this
world, but let God transform you into a new
person by changing the way you think.*
—Romans 12:2 NLT

This fifth one is also one of my favorites, because just as you can be excessive in praying in tongues, you can be excessive in the Word of God. If you want to pick a fight with the devil, if you want to start a war, you need to overeat the Word of God. As you know, Jesus was the bread that came down from heaven, the manna like they had in the Old Testament. When we eat of the Word of God and eat and eat and when we always put the Word of God before our eyes and ears, then we will be transformed. We should continually meditate on the Word of God, which causes us to think differently. We frame our world in our minds with the Word of God.

Jesus wants us to think about Him constantly. He is the Bread of Life, and we need to eat the Word. So we should not only think about Him but take in the Word of God and meditate on it. We must let it go deep down within us because it is a spiritual experience. For years, I have done this by taking one Bible verse and thinking about that verse all day long.

"And so, dear brothers and sisters, I plead with you to give your bodies to God because of all he has done for you. Let them be a living and holy sacrifice—the kind he will find acceptable. This is truly the way to worship him. Don't copy the behavior and customs of this world, but let God transform you into a new person by changing the way you think. Then you will learn to know God's will for you, which is good and pleasing and perfect" (Romans 12:1–2 NLT).

Paul says that the only way to worship God for all He has done for you is to give your body to Him as a living and holy sacrifice. That is what pleases God. And do not copy the world's behaviors and customs but let God transform you into a new person by changing the way you think. Then you will learn to know God's will for you, which is good and pleasing and perfect. I know that's what you want, and you can do this by overeating the Word of God.

You eat the Word like loaves of bread, constantly thinking about Jesus and about Father God. Think about the battle strategies that God has given you for your life. Think about what He is saying and doing and what your angels are doing. Constantly meditate on all the Word that has been given to

TAKING A STAND
AGAINST THE ENEMY

you in the Bible. When you do this, it starts to ignite something inside you, and that fire begins to burn. Then your mind is framed, and you start to be transformed, transformed by the renewing of your mind. You will be changed into a new person.

Your spirit is born again and on fire because you have accepted Jesus. The Holy Spirit revives your spirit. However, our soul is a different part of us and needs to be transformed as well. It needs to be renewed. Your soul is your mind, will, and emotions, which does not get saved. Your spirit gets saved, as it says in 2 Corinthians 5:17. You are a new creature, but your soul needs to be changed. You can have your behavior changed and transformed and become a new person by overeating the Word of God.

Jesus even spoke about overeating the Word of God. When He was in the desert with the devil, He picked a fight with the devil right there. After fasting, Jesus was hungry, and the devil said to Him, "If you are the Son of God, command that these stones become bread." Jesus said, "It is written, man shall not live by bread alone, but by every word that proceeds from the mouth of God" (Matthew 4:3–4). You have to crave and desire God and what He is saying more than anything else. If Jesus said this to the devil, then this is what you need to do. If you want to start a war, meditate on the Word of God.

In Matthew 13, Jesus talks about the parable of the sower. Some of the seed fell on hard ground, and the birds came and devoured it before it could take root. Jesus referred to this situation as the devil immediately coming in to steal the Word. Beware as satan will come and try to steal that from you when you do any of the following: hear the Word of God, think about the Word of God, hear a sermon, read the Bible, or meditate. I have seen this happen for years.

I have walked with the Lord for over forty years now. Some things haven't changed much. The devil knows when he is about to fight you in a war that he cannot win because you have the Word of God. The devil knows that he has to take that from you. He has to somehow pluck that Word out of you, but don't let him do it. You have to stand your ground and guard the seed that has been sown in your life. Always be mindful of what the enemy wants to steal from you.

"The thief does not come except to steal, and to kill, and to destroy. I have come that they may have life, and that they may have it more abundantly" (John 10:10). Jesus came to give life and life more abundantly. The thief comes to steal, kill, and destroy. Do not let him do this. I am telling you, I have seen this in the four decades I have been a Christian. If I overeat the Word of God, if I am constantly feeding myself with it, it starts a war with the devils that they cannot win.

No matter what you go through, continue to do what is right. You have to know that you are being attacked and persecuted for your stand for the truth. Still, you will always win because when the Lord starts a fight with the devil, He knows you can win against him. As long as you stay on track in the Word of God and in the Spirit of God, the devil will not win.

TAKING A STAND
AGAINST THE ENEMY

PRAYER

Father, in the name of Jesus, I thank You for the power that has been given to us by the Holy Spirit. I thank You for the blood of Jesus, and I thank You, Father, that right now, all my friends everywhere are sensing Your presence and powerful ability and that You are the true Word of God, Jesus. You came down from heaven as the Bread of Life. I thank You, Father, that You are working powerfully in us and that nothing is impossible if we believe.

Jesus, You told us that we are to eat Your flesh and drink Your blood. You are talking about a spiritual transformation that happens when we take every word that You said. The Holy Spirit ignites it in us, and it then releases life and transformation. We receive that transformation right now in Jesus's name. Ignite us by the power of the Holy Spirit. Thank You, Father. Amen.

What did the Holy Spirit reveal to you regarding this chapter?

TAKING A STAND
AGAINST THE ENEMY

Invoke the Name of Jesus

7

*Therefore God also has highly exalted Him
and given Him the name
which is above every name.*
—Philippians 2:9

The sixth way to start a war with the devil is by invoking the name of Jesus. The name of Jesus is the most powerful name that can ever be spoken. Did you know that the worldly media will block out the name of Jesus because evil spirits are paralyzed when you use His name? Jesus has been given the name that is above all names, and at the name of Jesus, every knee shall bow, and every tongue will confess that He is Lord.

"Therefore God also has highly exalted Him and given Him the name which is above every name, that at the name of

Jesus every knee should bow, of those in heaven, and of those on earth, and of those under the earth, and that every tongue should confess that Jesus Christ is Lord, to the glory of God the Father" (Philippians 2:9–11).

When we want to start a war with the devil, we can invoke the name of Jesus. Many times, I have seen the power of Jesus's name when dealing with evil spirits. I have dealt with demons inside and outside people, and when I have spoken the name of Jesus, it paralyzes these spirits. They literally cannot do a thing when you invoke the name of Jesus. The demons have to listen to you, so you should speak His name all the time.

It does not matter if you only repeat, "Jesus, Jesus, Jesus, Jesus." When I pray, I keep speaking Jesus's name until the devil starts to leave. At times, satan has tried to oppress me, come against me, or tried to get me to doubt or fear. But simply speaking Jesus's name is enough, and the devils will have to back off. You must know this.

This analogy will help you understand how speaking the name of Jesus works. Imagine you are in a building with a box on the wall that says "in case of emergency break glass." If you want to pull the fire alarm or reach for a fire extinguisher, you have to break the glass first. Then you can reach in and pull the fire alarm or grab the device. For us, His name accomplishes the same thing. I use the name of Jesus in case of an emergency. If all else fails, I will call out His name, which will paralyze the enemy every time.

TAKING A STAND AGAINST THE ENEMY

This name was used throughout the book of Acts. At the sound of that name, people were healed and delivered. At that time in the New Testament, the church was being built up, and people were coming to the Lord by the thousands. People who were persecuting the church took note that those people who had been with Jesus would always invoke His name. (See Acts 4:16–17.)

The authorities would pull the Christians in and beat them and tell them not to speak or teach in Jesus's name anymore. (See Acts 4:18–20.) After the Christians were beaten and threatened, they would come back and pray together and ask God to baptize them with boldness. They wanted to continue to speak and preach His name with even more boldness.

"'Now, Lord, look on their threats, and grant to Your servants that with all boldness they may speak Your word, by stretching out Your hand to heal, and that signs and wonders may be done through the name of Your holy Servant Jesus.' And when they had prayed, the place where they were assembled together was shaken; and they were all filled with the Holy Spirit, and they spoke the word of God with boldness" (Acts 4:29–31).

Wherever you go, remember this, especially if you are going to a new territory. When I worked for the airline industry, I was in a different city every hour. Our airline regularly did one-hour flights. We flew to a different city every hour, and I traveled to four to six cities a day. I stayed overnight at the last city and then started again in the morning and did another four to five flights the next day.

Every time we stopped, I was in a different state. I was going from territory to territory. I had to invoke Jesus's name in each territory because those devils stayed in that particular area. They were territorial and did not follow me around. I landed in a city and went through warfare in that city at the airport. Even if I were only on the ground for a half hour, I encountered different territorial spirits than from the previous city. I had to mention the name of Jesus a lot in my prayers to myself.

The people I met in between cities did not even know that I was battling with territorial spirits. If they were not Christians, my coworkers had no idea what was going on spiritually. (You might even relate to this.) I was in a different city every hour and at a different hotel every night. I had to regularly invoke the name of Jesus because I had to tell those spirits that I was a Christian and that I came in the name of Jesus. As an ambassador, I let them know that the hotel was my hotel now and that I was there in that city, taking dominion over those powers.

I spoke the Word of God out loud and preached and prayed in my room. Then I talked to my coworkers and people in the hotel, and I witnessed to them. I was doing warfare all the time. You will start a war with the devil simply by showing up. So you might as well use Jesus, the name above all names, and let all those devils know that you come as an ambassador of Jesus Christ on His behalf. You represent Him. When you invoke His name in a territory, I guarantee

TAKING A STAND
AGAINST THE ENEMY

that you will start a war with the devil. But it is a war you can win.

Sometimes when I talked to people, a growl would suddenly overtake that person. Sometimes a man's voice would come out of a woman. These evil spirits came right up and confronted me, telling me not to talk to this person. They said all kinds of strange things, and I told them to shut up, and then I would talk to the person about Jesus.

The demons were talking through that person because they were offended that I was there. They wanted me to leave the person alone because they did not want to lose that person. I told those evil spirits that they had to leave in the name of Jesus, and they would flip out. The demons told me they had to listen to me, and they did not want me to speak His name anymore. Those devils said it was a very powerful name and that they had no choice but to go.

I am encouraging you here by sharing what I have gone through over the years. If you even travel from one county to another (or parish where we live), you will find different sections and territories in your state. Evil spirits adhere to the boundaries of the different counties and territories. When Jesus was on earth, He ran into these evil spirits all the time, and they begged Him not to send them out of the area. "Then Jesus asked him, 'What is your name?' 'My name is Legion,' he replied, 'for we are many.' And he begged Jesus again and again not to send them out of the area" (Mark 5:9–10 NIV).

The demons are assigned to a certain area, and they do not want to leave because they are operating in the spirit world there. They have boundaries with a governmental order set up, and they do not want to be kicked out because it messes up their whole agenda. So you need to drive them out. You need to be aware that you might be crossing spiritual boundaries when you go from place to place. Certain people you meet will act up in resistance to your presence. Suddenly, you will see people be affected by these evil spirits as you are talking to them. You will encounter some very strange things because territorial spirits are involved.

You will encounter all kinds of changes in the spiritual environment as you move about your day. When you go to work, you will encounter different things than you did at home. If you are in a hotel room, you need to say the name of Jesus and bind evil spirits there so they do not bother you. You can even go to your church and encounter a religious spirit, and all of a sudden, people start acting up and talking strangely. You have to understand this and be sensitive to what is happening. Remember, you can win this war with the devil.

Do not be afraid to start a war with the devil by mentioning the name of Jesus as much as possible. Do not be bashful about it. God will give you the boldness to speak and preach the name of Jesus and the good news of the gospel everywhere you go.

TAKING A STAND
AGAINST THE ENEMY

PRAYER

Thank You, Father, for the impartation from heaven to learn about the power and authority of the name of Jesus. The Spirit of God can reveal truths about the name of Jesus to us and how powerful that name is. For at the name of Jesus, every tongue will confess, and every knee will bow, and every evil spirit will obey. I break the power of the enemy over every friend right now, and I drive out every evil spirit from all my friends all over the world in the name of Jesus.

I thank You, Father, that the Holy Spirit is revealing to us everything that we need to know about the name of Jesus. I thank You, Father, that right now, the power of the Holy Spirit is overcoming you. The power of the Holy Spirit is showing you how the name of Jesus is the name that is most powerful and that all things must come into order in your life in His mighty name. Amen.

What did the Holy Spirit reveal to you regarding this chapter?

TAKING A STAND
AGAINST THE ENEMY

Always Talk about the Blood of Jesus

8

*For you know that God paid a ransom to save
you from the empty life you inherited from your
ancestors. And it was not paid with mere gold or
silver, which lose their value.
It was the precious blood of Christ,
the sinless, spotless Lamb of God.*
—1 Peter 1:18–19 NLT

Another way you can start a war with the devil is by talking about the blood of Jesus. We need to strongly emphasize the blood of Jesus and Christianity because of the fall of man. The fact that we were kicked out of the garden was just the beginning. God warned us about the seed of the serpent. But the serpent's offspring Jesus would bruise the heel of the man-child that the woman birthed. "And I will put enmity (open hostility) Between you and the woman, and between your seed (offspring) and her Seed; He shall [fatally] bruise your head, and you shall [only] bruise His heel" (Genesis 3:15 AMP).

The Savior, the Messiah, was coming through the womb of a woman, and the seed or the offspring of the devil would bruise His heel. But Jesus would strike his head and crush the seed of the serpent. From the beginning, we have had this war going on that God foretold in the garden of Eden. God said that the seed of the serpent would come against the seed of the woman, but that the seed of the woman, Jesus, would win.

We have many genealogies throughout the Bible, but if you trace them all, you will see that the seed of the woman was never corrupted. However, there were many opportunities for this to happen, as we learn in Genesis 6:4 regarding the hybrid race. Interbreeding happened again after the flood, and a hybrid race popped up more than once. (See Numbers 13:32–33.) The seed of the serpent entered the human genome or human genetics. "For the life of the body is in its blood. I have given you the blood on the altar to purify you, making you right with the Lord. It is the blood, given in exchange for a life, that makes purification possible" (Leviticus 17:11 NLT).

Only eight people were on the ark, and they were perfect when they entered—perfect in their generations and in their genetics. (See Genesis 6:9.) That is why the law in the Old Testament says that life is in the blood. Since life is in the

TAKING A STAND
AGAINST THE ENEMY

blood, we have to keep it from being corrupted by keeping it pure.

Jesus kept the bloodline pure as the pure and spotless Lamb. That means that none of the genetic flaws from the reptile, from that serpent, could enter the lineage of Jesus. For this reason, the Bible lists all the lineages and the genealogies. They prove that Jesus was a perfect human being without spot or blemish and that He was the perfect Lamb, slain from the foundation of the world. Jesus's blood was pure.

"Knowing that you were not redeemed with corruptible things, like silver or gold, from your aimless conduct received by tradition from your fathers, but with the precious blood of Christ, as of a lamb without blemish and without spot. He indeed was foreordained before the foundation of the world, but was manifest in these last times for you" (1 Peter 1:18–20). "And the angel answered and said to her, 'The Holy Spirit will come upon you, and the power of the Highest will overshadow you; therefore, also, that Holy One who is to be born will be called the Son of God'" (Luke 1:35).

The Bible tells us that God was the Father of Jesus because the Holy Spirit came upon Mary, who became pregnant by the Holy Spirit. Jesus was fully God and fully man, and He was perfect. He never sinned, and His genetics were not flawed. When He presented His body as a living sacrifice, God accepted it. (See Hebrews 10:12–14.)

When God accepted Jesus's living sacrifice, we were forgiven of our condition of sin and of any future sin we would commit. From that point forward, we could rely on the blood of Jesus and ask for forgiveness. As we continue to walk with Him, He continually cleanses us because we are actively walking with Him and recognize and mention the blood all the time.

When I mention the blood of Jesus while dealing with evil spirits, I start a war. The evil spirits flip out every time, just like when I mention the name of Jesus. I have had evil spirits scream at me, "Please don't talk about the blood that destroyed us. The blood destroyed us and brought us to nothing." They were pleading with me not to mention the blood of Jesus, but I was only more excited to speak about it. I am telling you that we need to constantly talk about the blood of Jesus.

Our salvation is based on blood. In the Old Testament, animal sacrifices were given for our sin, but that just pushed sin to the cross. All those sacrifices, given year after year, could not completely take care of the sin problem. They postponed the punishment for the sin, which is discussed in Hebrews 10:1–10.

The book of Hebrews explains that the blood of goats and lambs could not forgive sins but simply put off addressing it until Jesus came. Once He came, that was the end of sin. We now rely on that blood, and I am telling you, this will wage war with the devil. If you focus on the blood of Jesus and talk to people about it, you will see evil spirits act up. You must be aware of this, but you cannot back off.

TAKING A STAND
AGAINST THE ENEMY

You must talk about the blood but know that it will start a war. You can go ahead and initiate it because the blood of Jesus will paralyze the enemy. Everything written about you in heaven will happen because the blood will stop the devil. You have to plead the blood over your house, your car, your children, yourself, and everything you do. I pray the blood of Jesus over everything I do, including Spirit School, Warrior notes, and the building. Everything is protected and set apart as holy by the blood of Jesus. You must do this every day, and I do not go a day without acknowledging the blood of Jesus.

I am forgiven for all my sins and feel that forgiveness as well. Why? Because the blood speaks. Remember when Cain and Abel were outside the garden, and Cain had not obeyed God as far as the sacrifice was concerned. (See Genesis 4:1–16.) His brother Abel had done the right thing and had sacrificed the firstborn of his flock. The Lord accepted Abel's sacrifice but not Cain's.

As required by God, Cain needed to make a blood sacrifice as well, but he did not do the right thing. He brought another type of offering, the fruit of the ground. Then God showed up and tried to coach Cain into obeying Him. The Lord said to Cain, "If you do what is right, will you not be accepted? But if you do not do what is right, sin is crouching at your door and desires to have you, but you must rule over it" (Genesis 4:7 NIV).

That is what the blood of Jesus does; it masters sin and everything that needs to be set right in your life. You need to be sanctified and set apart by the blood of Jesus. Then you need to have the power of the blood, the power of forgiveness, the power of sanctification, and the power that keeps you free of demons. Once you apply the blood of Jesus, satan cannot touch you because he cannot go through the bloodline. So you must always acknowledge the blood.

When the Israelites were slaves in Egypt, they lived in Goshen. When the plagues swept across Egypt, they never came near the Israelites. When the last plague, the death of the firstborn, came, God told the Israelites to put the blood of an unblemished lamb on their doorpost in Goshen so the plague would not affect them. (See Exodus 12:1–13.) Think about that. The Israelites had to apply the blood.

Now, all the other plagues never came to Goshen; they only came to Egypt. That was the only plague where God told them to sacrifice a lamb in each house and put the blood on their doorposts. Why did God require that? It was because we see the same principle in the New Testament. We need to apply and acknowledge the blood and mention it all the time. When we do, we will see protection like never before.

I often talk to ministers and have heard many stories about demon spirits sent by witches in their cities. One pastor said that demons were being sent to their church. The witches said that the spirits would come back to them and say, "We can't get into the building because they applied the blood. So we can't get in. We can't mess with that church."

TAKING A STAND AGAINST THE ENEMY

When the demons gave up, the witches came to the church and couldn't do anything. Then the head satanist came and sat in the church, and he got saved. When he got saved, he told the congregation everything. He said the evil spirits that worked with him could not do what he wanted them to do because the congregation had applied the blood of Jesus to the walls, and they could not come in.

That is the secret to waging war with the devil. When you start a war with the devil and mention the blood of Jesus, it is a barrier. You can stand behind the stronghold of the blood of Jesus.

The blood of Jesus applied to your life has a voice and has already spoken. After Cain killed his brother Abel, God asked him where his brother was, and Cain said, "I do not know. Am I my brother's keeper?" And God said, "What have you done? The voice of your brother's blood cries out to Me from the ground." (See Genesis 4:9–10.) Blood has a voice, and the life of the body is in the blood. Think about this. Jesus's blood is speaking right now on your behalf. You are forgiven, and you should never let the devil lie to you or steal from you.

PRAYER

Father, in the name of Jesus, I thank You so much that the Spirit of God is imparting this reality to all my friends everywhere so that they understand and grasp the truth and power of the blood of Jesus. Teach them that Jesus's blood has set them apart and completely taken care of the sin problem. Remind them that they are forgiven, that the blood of Jesus keeps devils away, and that the devil cannot wage war against the saints when the blood is applied.

Father, we apply the blood on all my friends worldwide right now as they listen to Your Spirit speak to them and receive this reality. I thank You, Father, that the blood of Jesus conquers and completes everything in a person's life. Thank You that all my friends are complete in Jesus Christ because of the blood. Thank You for it, in the name of Jesus. Amen.

TAKING A STAND AGAINST THE ENEMY

What did the Holy Spirit reveal to you regarding this chapter?

TAKING A STAND
AGAINST THE ENEMY

Allow God's Heavenly Strategies to Be Implemented in Your Life

9

*That the God of our Lord Jesus Christ,
the Father of glory, may give to you the spirit of
wisdom and revelation in the knowledge of Him,
the eyes of your understanding being
enlightened; that you may know what is the hope
of His calling, what are the riches of the glory of
His inheritance in the saints.*
—Ephesians 1:17–18

This eighth way to start a war with the devil is very important to me. In heaven, I saw strategies given to the angels in the command center there. Jesus was the head of angel armies, and He was telling the angels His strategies, which are planned ahead of time. All of us have things written about us in heaven that we should accomplish on earth, but we need help from the other side. Angels are sent to help us. If we allow God to implement His plan in our lives, we will be undefeatable. We can wage an effective war with the devil if we allow those heavenly strategies to be activated in our lives.

You need to go after it and say, "Father, I want everything that You have for me, and I want all of it implemented. I want to see the manifestation of God in my life." In this way, you will produce fruit that lasts as Jesus talked about in John 15, and you will see results. However, when God gives you these strategies, you must start applying them in your life.

Throughout the whole Bible, we read so many stories where God shares His strategies with those on earth. Think about the strategies that He gave Moses and how he had to implement them even though the people resisted him. Moses himself went up on the mountain with God and had all these amazing encounters and supernatural visitations for forty days. (See Exodus 19, 20, 24, and 34.) The people would stand back and would not engage God on their own at all.

Joshua was the only one who stayed with Moses the whole time. Even when the tent of meeting was built in the camp under God's direction, God gave the people another chance to meet with Him, but they refused. (See Exodus 33:4–11.) The Israelites wanted to let Moses do it. Besides Moses, only Joshua would continually be in the tent of meeting and would not leave. Joshua was face down in the presence of God in the glory that came from the pillar of fire. The cloud

TAKING A STAND
AGAINST THE ENEMY

by day came to the tent of meeting, and Moses and Joshua stayed in there for a long time.

I want you to picture what would happen if you allowed God to give you heavenly strategies and if you then implemented them, just as Moses and Joshua did. You would start a war with the devil, which would be positive. Moses was one of the greatest men who ever lived for God. And Joshua picked up where Moses left off and became the next great leader of the Israelites.

Joshua went in and took all those cities for God. He entered the promised land, taking millions of people with him. They all settled in that same land we have today, which is Israel. However, Joshua allowed God to activate all those strategies. God spoke to Joshua and let him know that Moses was dead, but Joshua would now take the people into the land that God was giving them. (See Joshua 1:1–9.) God told Joshua that no man would be able to stand against him all the days of his life. As God was with Moses, God would be with Joshua, and Joshua did as God directed. "'For I know the plans I have for you,' declares the Lord, 'plans to prosper you and not to harm you, plans to give you hope and a future'" (Jeremiah 29:11 NIV).

What has God been speaking about to you? What is your assignment that all the angels know you are supposed to do? No matter how the devil is coming against you right now, God has amazing plans and an expected end for you. He wants you to prosper in all that you do. He has already determined that you will end right.

When the Lord sent me back after I died on the operating table, He appeared to me and visited with me. He told me if I went back and told the people about all the wonderful plans He has for them, it would reroute their lives. People would change how they ended up, and they would finish strong. I am telling you what Jesus said to me.

You probably have many heavenly strategies that you want released and given to you, but you must implement them. You must engage God every day and pray the mysteries of this in the Spirit. You must speak to your mountains with your mouth so that they are removed. (See Mark 11:23–24.) Be like Joshua and go in and conquer those cities.

As Joshua went north into the promised land, he conquered all those pagan cities and drove out all the hybrid giants that were not supposed to be there. We should be doing this as well. We should be implementing those heavenly strategies in our present generation.

I was sent back to speak to this generation to encourage them to go the right direction by the Word of God, to encourage His children to remain *with* the Word of God and the Spirit of God to stay alive, full of life, and full of resurrection power. This is especially important in this time when people want to back off. The Lord gave me this strategy from heaven and placed me in this generation to speak the gospel to people. Even the next generation will hear this and will pick it up and carry on where we left off.

TAKING A STAND
AGAINST THE ENEMY

We will do our part, and then the next generation will do their part. At some point, when the harvest comes in and when all the people on the earth have had a chance to hear the gospel, the end will come. Matthew 24 addresses this. Jesus said that the end would not come until the gospel was fully preached, and then He would come back.

"Asking God, the glorious Father of our Lord Jesus Christ, to give you spiritual wisdom and insight so that you might grow in your knowledge of God. I pray that your hearts will be flooded with light so that you can understand the confident hope he has given to those he called—his holy people who are his rich and glorious inheritance. I also pray that you will understand the incredible greatness of God's power for us who believe him" (Ephesians 1:17–19 NLT).

We need to ask God that the eyes of our hearts would be flooded with light and that we would have the spirit of revelation so that we would know the hope to which we have been called. We need to ask for the glorious light to release the strategies of heaven for us, whatever they are. I want you to know what God is saying to you. I might not know what He is saying, but I can tell you the framework in which He works, and I can pray for you. We will pray that you have eyes to see in the Spirit.

Right now, more revelation is coming forth than I have ever seen, and I have studied many moves of God and the people who were used of God. I have not seen this kind of move happening on earth the way it is happening now. We have more of an open heaven now than I have ever seen, and I can tell you, it is just starting.

A glorious move of God is only beginning with a healing and a deliverance wave coming. In time, your finances will turn around, and I see this coming. The strategies of heaven and of angels are coming to earth, and Christians will implement them. They will boldly say, "This is how it's going to be. I will live my life according to the will of God, which is the Word of God, and combine the Word of God with the Spirit of God." When the Word of God and the Holy Spirit come together, you become a true believer on fire with resurrection power.

When you start to hear about heavenly strategies from God, you start a war, and then the war intensifies when you start to implement those strategies because satan knows he cannot win. So find out God's strategies and then implement them. If you follow His strategies, the Lord will be with you in a mighty way. Remember that the power of the resurrection is inside you and that God's plan is always to win. He knows that you can win this war.

TAKING A STAND AGAINST THE ENEMY

PRAYER

Father, according to Ephesians 1, I thank You that You are the Father of lights and that You will give all my friends around the world a spirit of wisdom and revelation in the knowledge of You. By this revelation, they will know the hope to which they have been called, and they will know the inheritance that Jesus acquired for all of us in the saints. I pray that we would also experience and encounter the resurrection power of Jesus Christ, the same power that rose Him from the dead that is dwelling in each one of us as believers. Right now, we yield to that resurrection power that can quicken our mortal bodies and that can renew our minds and help us see, hear, and operate in all the heavenly strategies that have been given to us.

We thank You, Father, that You give us the ability to implement these—not just to hear the Word but to be doers of the Word. We know that the world will want to stop us and that evil spirits will not want us to implement these heavenly strategies, but we will start a war by walking out Your Word. We will show the world what we believe by what we do. We will put action to our faith and release Your glory, that same glory, Father, that You and Jesus shared, according to John 17, that You said we can share in as well. Father, glorify Yourself in the church of the Lord Jesus Christ right now in the name of Jesus. Amen.

What did the Holy Spirit reveal to you regarding this chapter?

TAKING A STAND
AGAINST THE ENEMY

Stop Trying to Be Accepted by the World

10

*Do not love the world or the things in the
world. If anyone loves the world,
the love of the Father is not in him.*
—1 John 2:15

The ninth way to start a war with the devil is to stop spending time trying to be accepted by the world. When I was younger, I always felt the pressure to be accepted. At a certain point, I realized that I needed to find out what I was on earth for and then do that. When I became born again, I realized that I had a purpose, value, and safety. However, I had to submit to God and do it His way, which meant that I could not just choose any career I wanted. Instead, I had to submit to God. Once I did that, I started to see that the world is under an evil power.

Paul said that we used to be this way before we were born again when we were in the world. We did what the spirit of the world wanted us to do, and we did not resist it. (See Romans 7:5.) Why do Christians want to be accepted by the world or be part of that system? It does not make any sense. When you are born again, you come under the power of the kingdom of God into the kingdom of light, and now you can resist the devil. (See Romans 8:1–6.) You could not resist the evil in the world before you were born again. "Therefore 'Come out from among them and be separate, says the Lord. Do not touch what is unclean, and I will receive you.' 'I will be a Father to you, and you shall be My sons and daughters, says the Lord Almighty'" (2 Corinthians 6:17–18).

As you grow and mature as a Christian, you realize how much your heavenly Father loves you. He has all these amazing books written about you. (See Psalm 139:16.) These things must be implemented in your life by the angels and by the Holy Spirit. You start to realize that you need to stand out from among the world and be separate. Paul was commanding the believers in Corinth to do that: stand out, be separate, and not be part of the world.

"If the world hates you, you know that it hated Me before it hated you. If you were of the world, the world would love its own. Yet because you are not of the world, but I chose you out of the world, therefore the world hates you. Remember the word that I said to you, 'A servant is not greater than his master.' If they persecuted Me, they will also persecute you. If they kept My word, they will keep yours also" (John 15:18–20).

TAKING A STAND
AGAINST THE ENEMY

"Blessed are you when they revile and persecute you, and say all kinds of evil against you falsely for My sake. Rejoice and be exceedingly glad, for great is your reward in heaven, for so they persecuted the prophets who were before you" (Matthew 5:11–12).

Jesus talked about this all the time, and He said that since the world hated Him, the world would hate us too. He said we would be rejected by the world and persecuted. He told us to rejoice when we were left out and intentionally excluded. Jesus said, "Great is your reward in heaven." You are following Jesus Christ, and you want to be separate; that is what holiness is. It is standing out and being counted by God among His people because you are part of the family.

You do not have to be accepted by the world, and if you try, you will waste your time because satan will never let you feel accepted. He hates you and all Christians, so be at peace. Resolve now that you will find out what God has for you.

"Your eyes saw my substance, being yet unformed. And in Your book they all were written, the days fashioned for me, when as yet there were none of them" (Psalm 139:16). If you meditate on all of Psalm 139, it talks about how God knows the future and how He has plans for us. He already saw your body being formed in your mother's womb and wrote a book about you. Verse 16 says that all your days were written in God's book before one of them came to pass. He watched your body being formed in your mother's womb, so He knows everything about you. He has already spoken for you. Why would you want to be accepted by the world and by the spirit of this world? You have been accepted by God, and you are to be separate.

Right now, take a deep breath and let the Spirit of God come into you mightily. Realize that God loves you. He has accepted you, and you do not need to prove a thing. God has mighty plans for you—huge plans—and He has given you many angels to help you. There are more than enough angels to go around, and you will receive help from heaven. The Holy Spirit is always willing to give you the victory.

"Now thanks be to God who always leads us in triumph in Christ, and through us diffuses the fragrance of His knowledge in every place" (2 Corinthians 2:14). Paul said that God always caused him to triumph in Christ Jesus. The Spirit of God was constantly causing him to triumph. "Yet in all things we are more than conquerors through Him who loved us" (2 Corinthians 2:14). You are a dearly loved child of God, and you are to be an imitator of Him as His dear child. (See Ephesians 5:1.) God is not trying to be part of the world system or trying to be accepted by the world. He is God, and we are his beloved children. As His children, we let God love on us and teach us, and we let Him give us the victory.

I want to encourage you, especially if you are a young person. You might not understand this yet, but I wish that somebody would have shared these truths with me. As Christians, we will be rejected by the world, and we are wasting our time by trying to be accepted. You only need to

TAKING A STAND
AGAINST THE ENEMY

do what God called you to do. Find out what that is and let that come up within you.

You are accepted by God, so you can let the world do what it does, but you do what God does. His kingdom is advancing at an extremely accelerated rate. God is ready to accomplish all the plans and purposes He has for your life. Don't ever doubt that you are very valuable, and we need you to do what you are called to do.

Paul talked about how every part of the body is important. (See 1 Corinthians 12.) You cannot tell one part of the body that they are not important because we need every part. We need to rely on each other. We need each other, so you must be faithful to what you have been called to do and never try to be something you are not. That is all I am asking you.

I will believe that there will be a huge impartation into your life when I pray this for you now. I am asking you and pleading for you not to spend any more time trying to be accepted by ungodly people and the ungodly system of this world. Your value was determined in heaven, and a book was written about you.

PRAYER

Father, I thank You for all my friends and that they have released their wills to You and that they trust You. So many amazing things have been written about them as I saw in heaven. Everyone has a plan, a purpose, and value, and You have already preordained these things in their lives. If people will believe in You, trust You, and ask for help, You will come powerfully by Your Spirit.

I break torment, and I break all kinds of lying devils. I break fear and doubt in the name of Jesus, and I break your power, satan. I know that God's people are causing a war that we win because they are not wasting any more time trying to be accepted by your world system, satan. We reject your world system, and we know that God's kingdom is more powerful. Father, I thank You that everyone feels accepted by You. I ask for that impartation to go forth right now in the name of Jesus. Receive God's love, and let Him love on you. You are accepted. What satan says does not matter because what God says matters. You are beloved, and God has received you in the name of Jesus. Amen.

TAKING A STAND AGAINST THE ENEMY

What did the Holy Spirit reveal to you regarding this chapter?

TAKING A STAND
AGAINST THE ENEMY

Walking in the Fear of the Lord

11

*The fear of the Lord is the beginning of wisdom,
and the knowledge of the Holy
One is understanding.*
—Proverbs 9:10

The tenth way to start a war with the devil is by walking in the fear of the Lord. When you walk in the fear of the Lord, you acknowledge God and that He *is* God and you are not. When you say that the Lord is awesome, He is all-powerful, and you worship and fear Him. That is the beginning of wisdom. The fear of the Lord is the beginning of wisdom, but this also has to do with holiness. The fear of the Lord is clean and holy so that you are set apart. Walking in the fear the Lord will cause you to walk like Enoch did on the earth. (See Genesis 5:24.) When you walk in the fear of the Lord, you will walk in holy fire.

Holy fire is the purifying part of God for this life on earth. In heaven, you do not need to be purified because you do not have your earthly body anymore. When you are born again and Spirit-filled and when you go to heaven, you have a new body. However, down here on earth, you need to walk in holy fire and be baptized with fire as well as with the Holy Spirit.

"I indeed baptize you with water unto repentance, but He who is coming after me is mightier than I, whose sandals I am not worthy to carry. He will baptize you with the Holy Spirit and fire. His winnowing fan is in His hand, and He will thoroughly clean out His threshing floor, and gather His wheat into the barn; but He will burn up the chaff with unquenchable fire" (Matthew 3:11–12).

John the Baptist clearly said that one was coming. His name was Jesus, and He would baptize you with the Holy Spirit and with fire. I want all the fire that I can get from the altar of God in my life because it burns off the chaff and everything that is hindering me.

"Now if anyone builds on this foundation with gold, silver, precious stones, wood, hay, straw, each one's work will become clear; for the Day will declare it, because it will be revealed by fire; and the fire will test each one's work, of what sort it is. If anyone's work which he has built on it endures, he will receive a reward. If anyone's work is burned, he will suffer loss; but he himself will be saved, yet so as through fire" (1 Corinthians 3:12–15).

TAKING A STAND
AGAINST THE ENEMY

Paul said that when they go on to be with the Lord, everything they have done will be tried by fire. Only gold, silver, precious stones, and what is of value that you did on earth will be preserved. Everything else—the wood, hay, and stubble—will be destroyed by fire because these things done in your life were not of the Lord.

If you want to start a war with the devil and you want to have the rewards of walking in this fire on the earth, it will take sacrifice. It will be a challenge for you because satan will resist you. He knows that he cannot win this war, especially if he encounters holy fire. If you fear the Lord and walk in the fear of God, you start to receive wisdom and understanding, and then holy fire will be your friend.

"Then one of the seraphim flew to me, having in his hand a live coal which he had taken with the tongs from the altar. And he touched my mouth with it, and said: 'Behold, this has touched your lips; your iniquity is taken away, and your sin purged. Also I heard the voice of the Lord, saying: "Whom shall I send, And who will go for Us?' Then I said, 'Here am I! Send me.'" (Isaiah 6:6–8)

As described in Isaiah, the coal taken from the altar fire will touch your lips and cleanse you. Your situation will change and shift, and you will be right, when a minute ago, you were not sure about anything. That is why we need to encounter the other realm, the holy things. We need to walk in the fear of the Lord, and then we need to ask to be baptized in that holy fire. We need to let it touch every part of us and then just let it burn out whatever is not right. You do not want those things anyway, so let the fire reveal them. Whatever is precious will stay.

"Then Moses went up, also Aaron, Nadab, and Abihu, and seventy of the elders of Israel, and they saw the God of Israel. And there was under His feet as it were a paved work of sapphire stone, and it was like the very heavens in its clarity. But on the nobles of the children of Israel He did not lay His hand. So they saw God, and they ate and drank" (Exodus 24:9–11).

This verse in Exodus describes how God came down on Mount Sinai on a sapphire platform. God could not touch the earth because He had cursed it as fallen. If God touched the earth, it would start to break apart and catch on fire. But in this situation on Mount Sinai, God came down halfway and stood on that sapphire platform. He was in full view of Israel, Moses, Aaron, Nadab, Abihu, and the seventy elders who came up and ate and drank there. The Lord let them look at Him and see Him on that sapphire platform.

When I was in heaven, I saw that sapphire platform; an area in the throne room was thick sapphire stone, on fire, with white flames coming up throughout it. The Lord told me that not everyone could walk on those stones. Only a believer who walked in holiness on earth as a result of their relationship with God could walk there. A believer who was only aware of their position in Christ could not walk there.

TAKING A STAND AGAINST THE ENEMY

To walk there, you had to be a person who had implemented the kingdom of God in holiness and who walked separate from the world, submitting to holy fire. It could only be a person who let themselves be baptized in fire and who walked in the fear of the Lord, which is the beginning of wisdom. That person would be able to walk on this fiery sapphire platform in heaven. The Lord told me that Enoch was allowed to walk on the sapphire because he had submitted to God and had walked in the fear of the Lord.

Enoch had set himself apart and was persecuted on earth. As a prophet, he prophesied right before the flood. The earth was a mess at that time. If you talk to Enoch when you get to heaven, he will also tell you that he saw the end come, according to what was written about him. He saw what would happen with the earth at the time of the flood, but he also prophesied about the second coming of Christ. We see this in the book of Jude 1:14–15.

Enoch got to walk on that fiery sapphire platform up in heaven, and we can, too, if we do what qualifies us while we here are on earth. You are not qualified to walk there based only on your salvation by the blood of Jesus with forgiveness of sins. People will receive certain rewards for walking in holiness and separateness in heaven. I personally got to go places as a reward for the sacrifices that I had made while I was on the earth.

On earth, I never did my own thing but did what God told me to do. This cost me something, and a record of it was kept in heaven. Since I continued to walk in the fear of the Lord and in holy fire on earth, I was allowed to walk on this sapphire platform in heaven. I saw that it was the hottest, holiest place there. This fiery sapphire floor was lit up with the power of the Holy Spirit. It had white flames and was the most beautiful blue thick gemstone. The devil fights me when I talk about the holy fire and the sapphire stone more than any other topic. So I am encouraging you on this last point, number ten, in how to start a war with the devil. This should be your ultimate goal.

"By faith Enoch was taken away so that he did not see death, and was not found, because God had taken him; for before he was taken he had this testimony, that he pleased God. But without faith it is impossible to please Him, for he who comes to God must believe that He is, and that He is a rewarder of those who diligently seek Him" (Hebrews 11:5–6).

We must believe that there is a God and that He is a rewarder of those who diligently seek Him. This verse is mentioned right after the author of Hebrews talks about Enoch. Jesus told me the same thing about the holy sapphire when I was in heaven. We need to understand that we will be rewarded if we seek God diligently and if we walk in the fear of the Lord, in holiness, and in the holy fire. I want you to grasp the realities of Jesus Christ, but I also want you to realize what He has done for you. He has given you the ability to walk in holiness and in the fear of the Lord. That is available to every believer, but it goes beyond salvation because people must choose to do it.

TAKING A STAND AGAINST THE ENEMY

"Enter by the narrow gate; for wide is the gate and broad is the way that leads to destruction, and there are many who got in by it. Because narrow is the gate and difficult is the way which leads to life, and there are few who find it" (Matthew 7:13–14). When I was in heaven, I saw a narrow way and a wide way that led to destruction. You could barely fit through the opening in that very narrow way, and I saw that very few find it. I believe that you are receiving the impartation of the Spirit of God in this area to accomplish everything that God has called you to do. God is for you, but He is giving you a way to excel and go beyond.

"Follow God's example, therefore, as dearly loved children and walk in the way of love, just as Christ loved us and gave himself up for us as a fragrant offering and sacrifice to God" (Ephesians 5:1–2).

I want to do more than anyone else has ever done for God. I want to do the best that I can possibly do, and the only way to do that is to submit to the fear of the Lord, to holy fire, and to the impartation of the sapphire stone. That holy, heavenly blue sapphire stone is on fire in the throne room of God. I submit to walk on that and be like my Father God. I know I am not God, and neither are you, but we are to be imitators of God, as dearly loved children.

Jesus said, "If you can believe, all things are possible to him who believes" (Mark 9:23). Nothing is impossible if you believe, and I believe the best for you. I believe that you will receive the inheritance God has given you.

These are the ten ways that you can start a war with the devil that you *can* win. God bless you.

TAKING A STAND AGAINST THE ENEMY

PRAYER

Father in the name of Jesus. I impart all of heaven to each reader right now. I pray for all my friends to receive everything that can be given through Jesus Christ, including the fear of the Lord. I pray that they would receive the fire from the altar and that they would be baptized in fire. I pray that they would receive the invitation to seek You diligently and that You would reward them so that they can encounter the holy heavenly sapphire in the name of Jesus. Lord, touch them all, and I command every evil spirit to let go of them in Jesus's name. I thank You, Father, for giving us these ten ways to start a war with the devil that we can win, and we can win every single time. Thank You, Lord, for all my friends. Lord, baptize them right now in power. Heal their bodies and their minds. Restore them, Lord, and deliver them. Cause them to triumph in Christ Jesus just like You promised in the name of Jesus. Amen.

What did the Holy Spirit reveal to you regarding this chapter?

Made in the USA
Columbia, SC
18 March 2021